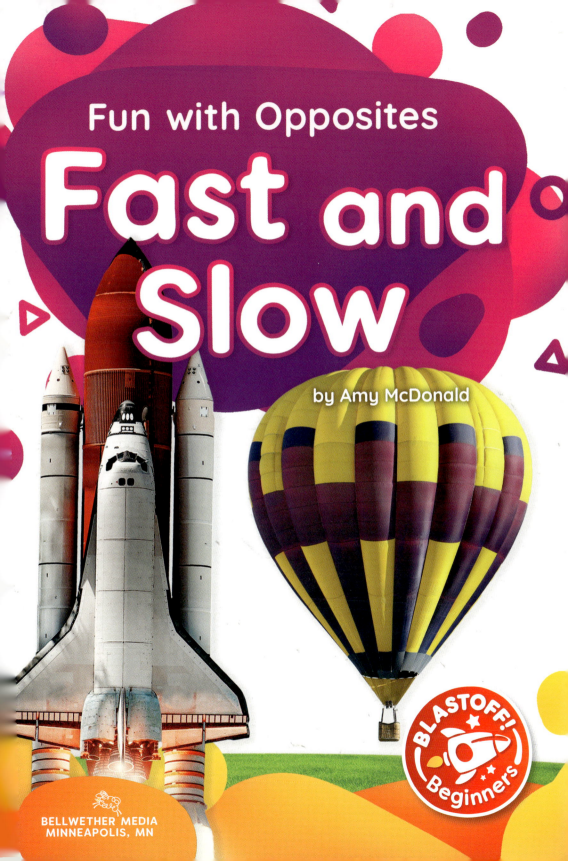

Fun with Opposites
Fast and Slow

by Amy McDonald

BLASTOFF! Beginners

BELLWETHER MEDIA
MINNEAPOLIS, MN

Blastoff! Beginners are developed by literacy experts and educators to meet the needs of early readers. These engaging informational texts support young children as they begin reading about their world. Through simple language and high frequency words paired with crisp, colorful photos, Blastoff! Beginners launch young readers into the universe of independent reading.

Sight Words in This Book 🔍

a	go	more	time	your
and	in	run	to	
are	is	the	up	
down	it	they	what	

This edition first published in 2026 by Bellwether Media, Inc.

No part of this publication may be reproduced in whole or in part without written permission of the publisher. For information regarding permission, write to Bellwether Media, Inc., Attention: Permissions Department, 3500 American Blvd W, Suite 150, Bloomington, MN 55431.

Library of Congress Cataloging-in-Publication Data

LC record for Fast and Slow available at: https://lccn.loc.gov/2025003237

Text copyright © 2026 by Bellwether Media, Inc. BLASTOFF! BEGINNERS and associated logos are trademarks and/or registered trademarks of Bellwether Media, Inc. Bellwether Media is a division of FlutterBee Education Group.

Editor: Rebecca Sabelko   Designer: Laura Sowers

Printed in the United States of America, North Mankato, MN.

Table of Contents

Lunch Time	4
Two Opposites	6
Fast and Slow Things	12
Fast and Slow Facts	22
Glossary	23
To Learn More	24
Index	24

Lunch Time

The worm is slow.
The bird is faster.
Lunch!

Two Opposites

Fast and slow are **speeds**.

Fast things go far
in a short time.

Slow things take more time to move.

Fast and Slow Things

Rockets **zoom** up! Hot-air balloons rise slowly.

Rain falls fast.
Snow floats
slowly down.

rain

Speedboats go fast.
They pass slow rowboats.

rowboat

Dogs run fast. Turtles walk slowly.

What is your
favorite animal?
Is it fast or slow?

Fast and Slow Facts

Fast and Slow Around Us

Something Fast and Slow

fast dog

slow turtle

Glossary

speeds

rates of how quickly things move

zoom

to go up quickly

To Learn More

ON THE WEB

FACTSURFER

Factsurfer.com gives you a safe, fun way to find more information.

1. Go to www.factsurfer.com.

2. Enter "fast and slow" into the search box and click 🔍.

3. Select your book cover to see a list of related content.

Index

animal, 20
bird, 4
dogs, 18
falls, 14
floats, 14
hot-air balloons, 12
rain, 14
rockets, 12
rowboats, 16
run, 18
snow, 14, 15
speedboats, 16, 17
speeds, 6
time, 8, 10
turtles, 18
walk, 18
worm, 4

The images in this book are reproduced through the courtesy of: Dima Zel, front cover; New Africa, front cover; Jakub Sisulak, p. 3; nexusby, pp. 4-5; Pete Stuart, pp. 6-7; AvokadoStudio, pp. 8-9; Damsea, pp. 10-11; Chris Carol, p. 12; NASA/Jerry Cannon/ Wikipedia, pp. 12-13; Lyudmila Lucienne, p. 14; Synthetic Messiah, pp. 14-15; Alberto Masnovo, p. 16; freevideophotoagency, pp. 16-17; Gerald A. DeBoer, p. 18; BIGANDT.COM/ pp. 18-19; Stu Porter, pp. 20-21; Sergii Figurnyi, p. 22 (top); Ammit Jack, p. 22 (fast dog); Jay Ondreicka, p. 22 (slow turtle); NASA/ Wikipedia, p. 23 (speeds); Soos Jozsef, p. 23 (zoom).